Testimonials

"In this penetrating yet soothing collection of streaming, rhyming, and repentant verse, the author maps his conversion from the shallow waters of grace to a life rooted in awe of a merciful and loving God. In it, he shows that what is most intimate and personal often has universal significance. In doing so, he challenges his readers to delve beneath the surface of their own lives, dive into the deep waters of existence, and allow them to penetrate their own hungry and thirsting souls."

– Fr. Dennis J. Billy, C.Ss.R.,
author of *My Journey's End* and other works

"Michael Sansone has become very close to God through contemplative prayer and faithful reception of the Lord in the Eucharist, as this collection of poetry attests. May his book have the same effect on you."

– Fr. Gerard Garrigan, O.S.B.,
author of *He Tells Stories*

"*Rhymes of Repentance* is a starkly tender pilgrimage through guilt, grace, and hope. With unguarded honesty and devotional courage, Michael Sansone offers luminous verses that feel prayed rather than written – inviting readers to face themselves before God and emerge renewed."

– Phillip Krill,
author of a series of books promoting a Trinitarian
vision of *Deification and Contemplative Prayer*

"There comes a time in a person's life when they look back to see what they have done and perhaps when they could have done differently. Upon review, some choose to do nothing. Some seek professional help risking a therapist who doesn't share their beliefs. Others, like Michael Sansone, turn to the roots of their faith, relying on God to guide them along the right paths. In this collection of poetry, Michael shares his very personal faith journey. He shows us what he has experienced and how all this has drawn him closer to the one God living and true. No doubt, as others prayerfully read through these poetic meditations, they will find something that will resonate with their own journey of faith."

– Father Dominic Lenk, O.S.B.,
author of *Voices from the Upper Room*

"A poetic examen of the soul, Sansone's verse draws readers into the sacred work of turning heartward toward Christ, where contrition becomes restoration and every honest lament flowers into hope-filled communion with God."

– Dr. Sebastian Mahfood, OP,
author of *The Narrative Spirituality of Dante's Divine Comedy*

Rhymes of Repentance

Michael Sansone

En Route Books and Media, LLC
Saint Louis, MO

En Route Books and Media, LLC
5705 Rhodes Avenue
St. Louis, MO 63109

Contact us at
contactus@enroutebooksandmedia.com

Cover Credit: Sebastian Mahfood using ChatGPT to reenvision Andrei Rublev's "Trinity"

ISBN-13: 979-8-88870-512-4
Library of Congress Control Number: 2026932538

TABLE OF Contents

Preface

In the final scenes of Spielberg's ***Schindler's List,*** Oscar Schindler is preparing to escape from the advancing Soviets at WWII's end. He laments on his sin of succumbing to his selfish pursuit of the world's material riches and self-indulgence over the needs and welfare of his fellow man.

As I approached my *winter years,* I began to identify with Oscar.

Although it borders on the extreme and melodramatic; nonetheless, I genuinely believed I could have done more to contribute to society, as an employer, husband, and a father to my children.

This was my ***PTSD*** resulting from over forty-five years as an entrepreneur, or so I imagined. The ***recommended professional cure*** was psycho medication.

As a cradle to grave Roman Catholic, now with adult responsibilities, I attended most Sunday, Holiday, and Holy Days of Obligation Masses. Now with a seniors' life crises upon me, I realized I was only in the shallow water of grace.

I chose a different approach. My cure became spiritual. I dove into deeper waters.

My doctors became the greatest healers known to humankind, Almighty God, His Son Jesus Christ, and the Holy Spirit.

I began to attend daily morning Mass, determined to never miss a day.

I went to confession as much as I needed and could bear and read many of the old Saints and Doctors of the Church writings.

Daily, I placed the burden of my guilt and sins at the foot of the cross below the sacred altar.

It was a slow and methodical recovery, lasting over two years.

Rhymes of Repentance is the result of the inspiration and graces of those two years of that determination, to seek and eventually experience a healing, no less miraculous as those revealed in the Gospels.

May it be The Holy Trinity's desire, that you, the reader, receive that same healing grace...

Turn the Page

In times trying
I often find myself
stopping my futile crying
on the frustration of circumstance
Of what now, what then, and what
  will pass
then upon the meaning and cause of
  it all
but then again more
Will others I know and love also fall

Those tales echo of old
true
loud
always and ever so bold
Is it the evil within or the evil without
which relentlessly keeps me so tight within its hold

This is the circumstance of which must be resolved
Before my bones turn eternally cold

Perhaps the blessed sage
has finally to convince
the solution is within
now it's time to no longer resist
so hurry
turn the page

MUSE

Every writer of word
music
theater
play
in thought will admit
but seldom say
mightier then sword
pen will not submit
to use
for forbidden it is
to speak openly
of a muse

The ever elusive
ever needed
very exclusive
necessary fairy
Is fleeting
staying rarely
very precocious
sometimes sad
seldom obnoxious
retaining good
as well as bad

Neither
demon
nor angel
what's sure
is to loose one
a writer will in oblivion
dangle

The Circus

Often times I wished
I had run away
and joined the circus
The Wild one
that to join
one does not pay

Unfortunately
in the mediocre one
I chose to stay
where one submits
one obeys
Never the thought
of foolishly running away

I've heard the stories
of those in the wild one
from the survivors who lost
not from those who won
Never revealing the cost
they paid to win the game
Bringing fortune
and fleeting fame
Was it paying half or whole
of ones precious immortal soul

Often I foolishly lament
but my cowardice I too
often compliment
that I chose to stay
avoiding the circus and
not running away

GRANDFATHER'S WORTH

I remember often when sleeping
at my grandparents
while mommy and daddy were
out and about
on the nights I seldom slept
Longing for them just short of
crying out
In a time I was two foot with
inches

no PJ's nor britches
but in diapers kept

A light from the kitchen drew me silently to see
My grandfather sitting at the head of the small table
On a chair one of three
In white strapped ribbed t shirt and boxer shorts
Intently reading
an old open book of tattered yellow pages
by old prophets and ancient sages

Curiosity compelled my toddler's finger
To reach up on tables edge to take a look
my gaze did not long linger
before he reached for me
His hand a soft hook
for a better seat I took

I sat nestled upon his lap
to read along
Especially where his finger did tap
"This you must learn
so far nothing else
You must earn
to overcome
all the obstacles of strife
that will come at you
often in this life.."

He saved me that night
teaching the wisdom
to win the inevitable fight

University

Decades ago
At the age of nineteen or so
I went to university
With the noble intent
To learn the cure for insanity
focused and hell bent
Don’t scoff
That’s truly why I went
For I to in mind was slightly
off

Senior photo in high school
yearbook quoted
Personal aspiration to be in the caption noted
A neurosurgeon
Impulsive words from still a virgin
But that I wanted to be
Search the archives
you’ll see
an historical fact you'll find
It’s true so it’s ok to laugh
I don’t mind
Impatiently in boring lectures I sat
Through tedious mundane
Repetitious this and that
More than half a year did I suffer
Couldn’t remember anything rougher

Resulting in a constant bad grade
I soon sought for another career to trade
Field trips to wards for the lunatic
taught only two cures for the mentally sick
Only coma drugs and electric shock
For futures fate I took immediate stock
To continue in this fruitless racket
I might end up in a straight jacket

So ended that future I dreamed
No further scheme to expropriate
For nothing inspired appropriate
Or so it seemed

My family and friends
Accused me of insanity
When for good
I left University

Vocation lost

Priests
the ones who stayed
true to His game plan
the ones who'll
receive all His treats
now and later
direct from
His loving hand

They're the winners
in this life
not the losers
as I was told
who couldn't
be bold
to brave a real man's
job of toil and strife
that made many
Sinners and boozers
as living took its toll

With the jeopardy of loosing
One's soul

Standing at the crossroads
of future wife
and seminary
the choices made
in the time of the passing sea-
sons
cloud the memory of any rea-
sons

Was it best
the one with whom
I stayed
Regardless His will
Be done
Perhaps
Staying true to that
I've Won

Cowboy Fear

I finally gotta hold of a girl I
used to know
She prefers to text
Not use voice
because it might show
the mood she's in
or hide what she might say next

She's older now
With grown kids
Not so easy to impress
or wow
Nor show
the tones & inflections of how
The human voice can soothe
Persuade, a point prove
or one's attention
loose
Much like the time of the Cowboy past
When a car first appeared
with the fear that the horse would never last

Home

That's the place from whence
we came
arriving here
We tried to make it the same

For years and years
We did what we could
Spending blood
Sweat and so many tears

That's the definition of insan-
ity
Succumbing to pride, arro-
gance
and foolish vanity

Bending knee
Begging
Seeking a reprieve
from the worlds trouble

Only to rise and make it dou-
ble

The child soon
became a man of old
Emptied of pride and arro-
gance
No longer bold
Whittled down so much
That with the here
we lost touch

Only now we understand
There's no need of a helping
hand
Because the we
was always only me
Not wanting here to roam
Patiently waiting on
a way to return home

Thor's Hammer

I'm as a
twisted piece of steel
Within these twists
they do conceal
my sins
faults
failures
and a few minor wins.

Upon God's anvil
on back I lie
graciously distracted
by the miraculous
stars in the night sky
Through its glamour
the sparks interacted
with the pounding
of the Archangel's Hammer

Within each spark
no longer hidden
the fruits which are said to be forbidden
my faults failures and sins
with few perceived wins

With each hammer pound
Loud thunder's rise

An echoing bellowing sound
That muffles my feeble cries
On all His miraculous wonders
From each strike of this holy hammer
Are rendered to an inaudible
Unintelligible stammer
in the Archangels mighty smithy hand
with incredible strength of wrist
Straightens every distortion
every twist

Now straight is this piece of steel
There no longer remains a place to conceal
Not even in a tiny pore
A sin, failure, or fault no more

Never underestimate
What evil may have in store
Upon its inevitable return
Just as before
To taunt
it's methods are to haunt

Should one fall or stumble
Trip and fall
Seek always to be humble

The faults, failures
The worlds glamour
To them do not submit

Nor to pride and vanity
Forever keeping one's faith
Ones sanity
All by enduring the pounding
Of the Archangels hammer

Upon God's anvil
On back I rest
Still yielding and grateful
The Archangel ended the test
From the world's constant clamor
I will not tire
For there's Thor's Hammer
Above
In the stars of Ursa Minor

WHAT-FINGER !?

Thunder echoes through my valley
after harsh lighting cracks
sparks senses reeling
Both mock and mimic
the thoughts I'm feeling

Ah, youth has past but it's thoughts still linger
as it laughs and shows me the middle finger

I'm stuck in the rut of life passing bye's
often dazed and confused
my restless spirit travels constant
through lows & highs

My senses return
as I realize I alone
am not yet left to burn
Many days are before me to languish and linger
If you scoff or protest to much
I will show you my middle finger!

Atmos

It's as a pop-up thunderstorm
on a blistering hot afternoon
so satisfying
it should be the norm

The lighting the thunder
stirs one's soul deep down
way done under

The rain precedes the wind
cooling and caressing
stirring one's soul
Deep within

The land the air
and all creation
thrives on the miraculous
Revelation
that Gods love
Is in everything
everywhere
always & not only from above

This infinite love is the mor-
tar
the magic that holds all mole-
cules together
despite the efforts of the dark
thwarter
to scatter and deceive
that we're the arbiters of all
even weather
not what our faith has us be-
lieve

Don't believe evils chaotic
tricks
Trinitarian Love is the mortar
of the cosmos
connecting its molecular
bricks
Forever preserving the divine
Atmos

SHEPARD'S MOON

I've a little cabin
in the woods
a quiet hermitage
surrounded by
a wild multi flora hedge
Near a spring fed stream
across from lush clover fields
a special place
as one sees in a dream

There our good shepherd kneels
tending His flocks
Where time matters not
No need of anything
not even clocks

It's a one window cabin
with a clap board door
and a very clean
packed clay dirt floor

No fancy furniture
nothing is required
nor need of any frivolous ex-
penditure
just a simple cot
by a little wood stove
only in winter or for cooking
kept hot
one small table
two chairs
Simple but stout and stable

This night
the forests shadows are dark
and long
but no cause for fret or fright
for the moon is big

full and very bright
pouring through the window
washing white the table
and clay dirt floor
with dazzling beams stream-
ing
from the cracks in the clap-
board door

As if in a trance
or on the edges of sleep
I hear gentle sounds
So Close
the soft the bleating of sheep
wearing tiny bells
with faint
tinkling tolls
In open doorway our Shep-
ard stands
with round red holes
in bare feet and open hands
I gaze in wonder and awe
wide eyed
with open slacked jaw
without any fear
as His outstretched arms
Beckons me near

St. Paul's Lament

For I do not do the good I want to do
but the evil I do not want to do—this I keep on doing

Safe in the realization
Paul of the Bible is a saint
There may still be hope
For my salvation
But what he was/is and did
I ain't
That's a fact that leaves no room
For the slightest debate

No penance will suffice
Short of self-flagellation
As the demon's lick their lips
And scratch their lice
Eager for my eternal damnation

I'd willingly take on Paul's heavy load
Of what occurred on the Damascus road
Three days of blindness
To madness was he driven
If all my sins
Like his were forgiven

The Obituary

It's in holy scripture what He said
that's verifiable factual and true
Even so
many don't believe
but some do
more than just a few

To follow Him
abandon all carnal behavior
all occasion to sin
to die from one's old life
and stay with our Savior

Humility

There's a subtle peace
acquiring a humble spirit
al be it's a difficult fit
as a too
small coat
or shirt
to wear it
although
once put on
it can be comfortable
like a victory
won

Should proper
fit diminish
Remain in the race
to its proper finish

Devil's Grenades

Dismayed and appalled
watching
the ICE riots in LA
one can only look
heavenward to pray

In holy Mass
we *mea culpa*
with *miserere nobis*
for assuredly
only He can save
and we fervently
know this

as our eyes occasionally
raise
pleading for solutions
with thanksgiving and praise

Distractions flood in
with a succession
of nonsensical tirades
much like the flash bang
anti-riot grenades
to disrupt and cause
confusion with
persistent diabolical
profusion

to overturn
and cast us adrift

In faith
we shake it off
In revelation of God's
grace
and greatest gift

Visions in Dreams

There appeared before me
a vision
a dream I could barely see
Behind the altar at the start of
Mass
like a renaissance painting
or a sculpture of gold
bronze silver and brass

Hovering above
a man's height high-in celes-
tial magnificence
forcing me to stifle a cry
upon realizing its significance
with a soft soulful sigh

Within billowing cloudbursts
celestial double doors so
bright
I had to squint to maintain
this vision
this sight
Perhaps of Ghiberti's creation
The Archangel Michael
does appear
only with drawn sword
No scales nor spear

made with priceless cost
without moderation
those of the Duomo in Flor-
ence
Alas the answer is lost
In the majestic harmony
of the angelic chorus
Guarding the closed door
until the priest celebrant
takes the floor

As Mass starts to begin
two blazing white Angels
pushing the doors from
within
moves St. Michael away
with no sound
no word
On altars right he will stay
hands upon sword
by its hilt above the T
With bowed head
on one knee
From fully open doors
misty golden light spilled
silhouetting faces
both joyful and thrilled
on the threshold
filling all available spaces

Staring at us all
the prayerful congregation
mimicking our prayers
our kneeling and standing
our responsorial conversation

As priest hands bless
for we've taken to heart
Christ's life
His attitude
wine and bread
those on the threshold
with awe gaze overhead
A most blessed sight to be-
hold

Through the light
of a thousand candles
comes the one
that none are worthy
even to untie His sandals

He through the priest
with The Holy Ghost
transform simple bread
into Sacred Host

This sacred mystery
Gift of Our Savior
by His arrival in history
forever altered
mankind's sinful behavior

Now at Mass end
with humble gratitude
one knee we bend

The doors close
signaling the world to start
with us from knee
St. Michael rose
to do our sacred duties
our sacred part
We chosen few
with Christs love
to help all the world anew

FACETIME

For a very long time
I've longed to see His face
many renditions
In all colors
In various conditions
To be absolute
sure
I've seen not even a trace
We've the Shroud of Turin
Revealing possibilities
Disguised by torture pain and
ruin

There's the
Salvador Mundi
Angelic
By da Vinci

They keep trying to convince
me
While in a heightened
State of grace
I kneel
pleading to see His face
He answers back
Clear
In truth
I do not
Lack
I'm everywhere
In every place
Every man
woman
especially a baby
You'll see
for sure
not maybe
with joy so pure
My face

Humble Pie

Pride &
arrogance
have been
my constant pain

Try as hard as I must
It's often in vain
my ignorance of solution
frequently ends in a bust
my efforts to change
always without resolution

Low and behold
now and then
Gods knows why
It is He
I'm told
served up
a slice of humble pie

Now
near the end
of my race
in the last bend
before the victors
Laurel did descend
the whole
Humble Pie
smashed in
my face[1]

[1] Inspired by the week old new car crash.

CONFESSION

Looking back on past woes
On friend's acquaintances
Colleagues and foes
It's become quite clear
Only pride and vanity
I didn't fear
As I should
The obvious cause of my in-
sanity
Not that I was able
Or even could

I was unwilling
Doubtful I would
Measure up to expectations
Using sweet words
and flattering salutations
Impressive Shakespearean wit
With manly tough
John Waynean grit
I used them all as a tool
As camouflage to hide the
fool

The ego errant used sinful
pander
While reveling
Gleefully
In delusions of grandeur

Like an off beat
Gong booming
A warped cymbal crashing
A delusional child
Whose only penance
is a good thrashing

PRAYER

We come before you humble
and contrite
Bowed head to take a knee
All the while avoiding Your
sight
Seeking healing of body
mind and soul
Our self indulgence
Has taken its toll
The weak us
we prostrate ourselves in
your divine presence.
of low spirit humble and
poor
remaining numb our spirits waiting for your forgiving love
Our prior sanctity to restore
Patiently with confidence
We remain open to your divine intervention

Dolan's Mistake

Today it became
crystal clear at the inauguration
in all we hold dear
the old Cardinal omitted
His holy name
and a sin he committed
as freedom was almost aflame
Alas old tradition caught fire
the current state of our reli-
gious condition
appears quite dire

the anemic sign of the cross
coupled with lack of mention
that Jesus is the boss
Squandered a holy tradition
evils perilously close
so pray much
avoiding the small dose

How do we make
an amend
to halt this
madding trend
of lacking devotion to
Almighty Gods will
rather that of man
for his pride to fill
we've no choice
but to hear reasons
of divine voice
warning to avoid
any weakness
but in wisdom
surrender to Jesus
and His meekness

** Inauguration Day 01/20/25*

African American Fire

He invoked His Name
The Father the Son
and the Holy Ghost
All one and the same

Rev. Lorenzo Sewell
Rang freedom's
Holy bell
Passionate
Loud and assuredly clear
For all mankind to hear
On that Inauguration Day
Blessing our nation he leads all
To fervently pray

Two other benediction presenters
So mundane timid and boring
Came close to being tormentor's
While Lorenzo's praises
Sent onlookers hearts and spirits
soaring

..thank God almighty we're free at last..

Echoed the cries of hero patriarchs
and freedom lovers who fought off

All tyranny of the past
By calling on the name of Jesus
With arms held up high
All who heard were speechless
On that Inauguration Day
When Rev, Lorenzo Sewell
Rang loud Freedom's bell
Aloft In the holy spire
Lighting all the world
With his blazing African American fire

Fat Tuesday

I've fallen
and can't get up

Often, we feel pity
And we might chuckle at evening sup
but what we must feel
Is to tighten one's buckle
Reach down
Plant the heal and help lift up
Dust off the gown
as He did
so many times
when I was about to drown

I've fallen
but there is no can't
I pray between every
Breathless pant
for His hand to lay hold of mine
to put me back on track
in no time

The Vincentians

I recently joined a club*
Not one that was heard of in a
pub
where old became young
Not by flattery
nor things of the tongue

Members need not know
from status
nor pedigree
whence they come
or how high the family tree
nor the accolades
from the pages of all the an-
cient
ages

With childlike abandon
they came to realize
and fathom
the precious words of our Sav-
ior
which forever altered our be-
havior
"..what you do to the
least of thee you do to me.."

One must not
linger nor stay silent
with lips under finger
when opportunities arise
to seize the ultimate prize
of planting the seed
of Christ's healing love
in all those
we serve
in their need[1]

* The St. Vincent De Paul Society.

An Old Tale

Long long ago, in a land far far away, in a time lost in history, there existed a land where a tribe of little people lived.

Although little, they were strong and prospered.
They defeated all enemies and lived in relative peace.
The Leader of the tribe was loved and honored by many.

He was a GIANT of a man.
Both in character and stature!
For many years and several generations he ruled well.
One day he passed away.
All mourned for him greatly.

In this land, the ancient rule of "Salic succession" fell upon the eldest male heir.
When the Giant Leader passed, his oldest son became the tribes leader.
Although taught and trained by the Giant Leader, he was not the giant of a man the leader was.
Nonetheless he was expected to fill the Giant Leaders shoes.
Not only did the tribe expect it, but he did as well.
All agreed it was his duty.

The only trouble was the Giant Leaders shoes were GIGANTIC!
So Gigantic, the new leader could not walk in them.
He couldn't even move without being scoffed and ridiculed,
So much so that his requests for order in the tribe were ignored.

Even when he demanded traditional rules of old be followed, many turned their backs on him and kept away.

He became so lonely and confused, his health, both mental and physical began to deteriorate.
Keeping those gigantic shoes on we're driving him down to self destruction.

Soon he dropped to his knees seeking absolution
when the gigantic shoes fell off!
He looked to the heavens and asked God Almighty for help and a solution.
God answered him – *FIND YOUR OWN SHOES!*

ANXIETY

Chest boulders
Emptied is a remedy for com-
plete closure
An antidote for the tightness
the boulder
Lying with accumulated
things trying best
To beat you by lodging deep
in the chest.

The heartache compels one
To sort them out
and when done
Flush them all away without
delusion
Returning to empty
the only solution

Staying empty is the key
Knowing there's no pleasure in that
Temptations whispers
that serpent in the tree
Cajoling the empty to once again fill
Like the Humpty Dumpty teetering on the sill
One must not look down fearing the fall
Look up eyes riveted on the prize
Ignoring temptations seducing call

Let the empty be filled by His light
Dissolving all boulders deep in the chest
Let all good angels keep up the fight
Now lay me down as a child in the night for rest

EGOMANIAC

Certainly my ego is
my ever constant Bain
Like being exposed
stark naked in a frigid blowing rain
Sinful judgements
Result in paradoxical
Punishments
For the Judge becomes what is judged
Ironically revealed
A fate so just
It can't be concealed

The ego one must despise
So a word of caution
to only the wise
To you I'm compelled to advise
Avoid it's constant temptation
If ever you hope to attain
eternal salvation

Full 4am Moon

We long for the song of the
whipper will
It calms our spirits
and keeps our hearts still
The low hoots of the night owl
refresh like the caress of a
warm wet towel
upon a soiled face
wiping away all
leaving nothing to blemish
not even the slightest trace

In solitude comes the quiet
peace
not that of this world
but of the spirit
Where the best become the
least

The morning full moon falling
Casts shadows of milky white
as creation praises its maker
for this fortuitous
miraculous sight
in songs of gratitude and joy
with a constant calling

In harmony our souls
join in the song
as distant soft bells toll
a faith filled reminder
with Him
nothing is wrong

PRESENCE

Now that I'm in,
perhaps my final decade,
blessings from heaven
upon me,
begin to cascade

As my pace quickens
on discarding worldly stuff,
alas, my stubborn hard head
thickens
Some stuff goes easy,
others go rough

If a priestly spirit perseveres
in vows of holy essence,
only then, one easily com-
mandeers
Jesus's holy Presence

Beware heaven's assumption,
for to do so may lead
to spontaneous combustion

Every minute,
take a deep breath
remembering the inevitability
of death
while clearing conscience
with belief in the heritability
of Jesus's Presence

Praying for Judas

After staring at this ti-
tle
for over a month
words compelled many
visits to the Bible
what didn't seem like
much
Became a literary gut
punch
Risking the scolding
critic's fate
As poor Judas brings
on so much hate

Justice for Judas is hard
Even for the most illus-
trious
most stupendous
and most industrious
lawyer bard

Can one argue
It was part of His plan
Deja Vue
as the French say
Involving the Son of Man
On the morning of the third day

Look again at the evidence
In order to solicit poor Judas
some recompense

For it is written
Jesus
Betrayed by a kiss
Not a slap
was He smitten

Our Lord did say
as a director to an actor in a play
for Judas to proceed with what is ordained
In haste stirred by greed for silver his betrayal was obtained

So pray for poor Judas
It's never too late
He left us to ponder
his tragic fate
Is it just
I'll always wonder
the last of his breed
he left no heirs
he planted no seed

is it just
I'll always wonder

Gelassanheit

As my years steadily advance
False Illusions no longer concealed
Place me in a trance
Past sins of control revealed
Painfully understood

Cherished beloved
sired brood
Keep their distance
with the lack of communication
Sad in its persistence
Their apparent apathy
Maybe a family catastrophe

I've no other choice
But lift up hands
To pray with my voice

Father in heaven
I trust in You
Seventy times seven
Forgive I must
For they know
Not what they do

** Gelassanheit: German for relinquishment, surrender, abandonment, submission, letting go, etc.*

Culprit's Current

History doesn't record
Or it's mystically forgotten
rightly and quite justifiably
The names of those misbegotten
Who scourged our Savior
Hammered nails in feet and hands
Pagan slaves from conquered lands
Conscripted and set free into the Roman Legions
Assigned to Judea's surrounding regions

Traditionally given names of Latin
by which they were called when it happened
Six men who committed that heinous crime
Of which they weren't aware at the time
Only following orders to which they below were assigned

Indulgentias
Self-indulgence

Confabulationes
Gossip

Rumones
Rumor

Superbias
Pride

Vanitas
Vanity

Invidias
Envy

Known then by their Latin
name
Now by English
ironically almost the same
Sadly these current culprits
performing evil old tricks
through time they haven't lost
Mainly on those who've taken up His cross

In the guise
of kin friend and foe alike
to the holy prudent and wise
to mock whip and hammer in the nail spike

Every day
With, in, and all around us
with impunity they prey
Alas, I fear
those six are still here
to stay and may never
Ever go away

LIMERICK FOR DOMINICK

We heard today
from a fellow brother
not of blood
but of another mother
not a sprint
but a marathon
you must run

It maybe brutal
and seldom fun
sometimes uphill
Which can seem
often futile
Carrying a ton
a heavy load
For around the next bend
of this twisted road
It levels out close to the end

So stay on the road
avoid the false trail
For many are cheering
you on to persevere
to prevail
You've all the grace
to win if you maintain
Gods will
His ordained pace
For many in history
have finished in
absolute victory[2]

---

[2] For my friend, priest, holy monk, mentor, and Dean of Theology, Fr. Dominic Lenk, OSB.

The Summit Meeting of Chaos & Order

The meeting took place recently in a secure location unbeknownst to all save this humble reporter.

Why I was chosen to be there remains a mystery so far.

Perhaps after this event is relayed to you. I will have time to investigate the cause of my good fortune, if that is indeed what it is.

I stood by the huge double doors of an immense hall , without a visible ceiling. As the main participants entered, it quickly became obvious there were two distinct groups which huddled to together as they filtered in.

There was commonality only amongst those in their group.

Each of the two groups were so different in appearance and manor that it was no chore to label them for narrative purposes.
Chaos was represented by sinister looking ones surrounded by a foreboding darkness.

They entered the empty hall, devoid of any seats, pushing and shoving each other without any purpose except for the sport of it.

Order came into the hall behind Chaos. A light surrounded them, enhanced by the clean appearance of their garments and a pleasant, calm disposition.

Both groups stopped, before a stage, keeping a wide open aisle between them.

Chaos on stage left.

Order on the right.

At the end of the participants procession were two giants.

Both giants were broad of girth, muscular, and as tall as four men each standing upon the others shoulders.

At first glance they appeared human.

Both wore hooded chain mail, extending to the hip and down their muscular arms secured by leather wrist greaves.

The giants stood in the doorway blocking any uninvited guests.

They waited in silent discipline for the procession to fill the area before the stage.

As the giants turned towards the entrance in unison, I saw one armed with sword and buckler.

The other with a rather large double bladed battle axe thrust into a wide silver belt.

Both had shields hung over their shoulders, covering their backs.

With obvious effort they began to shove the massive doors shut.

As each dug in their heels, I was amazed to see the edges of wings appear out from under the cover of the shields.

A thunderous echoing boom proclaimed the closing of those doors.

Each giant now took hold of a large wooden beam which had been leaning upright and hidden behind one of the open doors.

It was so huge, it took both giants to heave it up onto massive locking cleats bolted on each side of the tremendous doorjamb.

I marveled at the size of such a tree it must have been carved from.

Perhaps a tree from the old earth prior to mans expulsion from Eden?

During this brief fixation on the doors, I noticed it was designed to only open inward. A meaningless thought quickly forgotten for the time being.

A second and final boom reverberated through every bone in my body as that beam fell into its resting place.

Each giant turned and backed into the massive doors, faced the stage, nodded a silent pledge in unison that none now shall enter nor leave!

Like the giants, all turned to looked at the stage. Distracted by the door closing, I was unaware both groups had gone up onto the stage.

With the immense hall secure, it was clear to me all

were intent on beginning the meeting.

A delegation from each group sat down at the two tables . An elaborately carved stone podium separated the tables.

I took notice of how different each table was.

The left table was so pleasing to the eye that it was difficult not to stare.

Its bejeweled carvings of Satyrs and Griffins, were surrounded by both naked and scantily clothed women.

Naked men were frolicking with lions, foxes, large horned goats, and various exotic creatures.

The spectacular images beckoned this beholder to approach, and even though out of reach, to touch.

As I was about to do just that, this intoxicating impulse left me.

Now sober, I looked for the best way up onto that stage.

If there had been a way of getting on that stage, it was gone now!

Perhaps I was destined to be the sole audience?

While seeking access and reconnoitering my approach, my eyes were drawn to the right. To the contrasting table of Good.

As if drawn there by some unseen force, I stopped and stood a few paces back on the right side of that stage below this table.

This tables simplicity was oddly refreshing.
Seated quietly behind, were twelve men, all well groomed.

Some wearing robes of ancient times.

Of Pre Roman era, but more Hellenistic.

Perhaps Alexandrian before the conquest of Persia?

Two were clad in Gentlemen Gentry dress of the seventeen hundreds.

One in a Union Calvary officers uniform of America's civil war.

Seated next to him, a Sioux Warrior Chief in full headdress and beaded leather clothes.

One man in particular stood out from the other eleven.
His demeanor and aura insured He possessed absolute stage presence.
He was standing in Arabic style robes of white and gold.

These robes moved around Him as if by a light breeze, even though the air was as still as He.

It immediately became obvious the others looked to Him as their leader.

In contrast, the left table was occupied by thirteen, dressed in the current modern business tycoon and pop star fashion.

The best men's fashion designers from New York, Milan, Paris and London were all represented.

I moved closer.

My approach was ignored by all but one man, the leader of the Order table.

He walked around to the front of the simple table as if to greet me.

His face ordinary, not overly handsome, but pleasant.

Although he seemed to recognize me, i could not swear i had seen him before.

The noise from the left table reached such a crescendo that all eyes including mine were drawn there.

One darkly dressed man, more groomed and fit looking than the others at the table, spoke up from his still seated position.

"Well now, I see we are all here.

I know we of Chaos have much better things to do, so, lets proceed shall we!"

Those at his table showed obvious approval with affirmative body gestures, table knocking of knuckles, clipped guttural here here's, and clapping.

Those at the order table, without emotion, looked to their leader still standing on the stage up in front of me.

Without hesitation, He took position behind the podium and began to speak.

"Since these proceedings are of such a vital nature and your calls for urgency are equally felt by us as well, with your permission i will begin."

I was surprised by the rude guttural comment from the dark one.

There was now no doubt he was their leader.

He chuckled a sarcastic barb as he looked around among his constituents,
"Well, well, now, He knows He needs not my permission!"

Those at his table chuckled along with him.
He waved his multiple ringed fingered hand in the air and rudely continued,

"Yes by all means, begin!"

(Authors Note): For efficiency I will call the two leaders Good and Evil. It is simply my opinion. I leave final judgement to you my readers.

Public speaking is an art.

As Good began, it became quickly clear the infamous Roman, Cicero may have taught Him, or He, Cicero.

"It has come to our attention that the scales of our universe are no longer balanced.

Chaos is increasing in weight and popularity as Order begins to diminish.

If this trend continues, forces
beyond our control will
intervene placing all in
jeopardy!"

The Good leader was shouted
into pausing his discourse
by the protest from the
chorus at the table of
Chaos.

"Proof, proof proof!' They
chanted in unison.

The Good One kept his composure as he waited for
the chorus to subside.

"Proof you say?

How much proof do you require and how many millennia do you wish me to
expose the imbalances?

Cain & Able,
the Tower of Babel incident,
Noah and the flood?

Or perhaps the Crusades,
Spanish Inquisition,
Americas civil war, WWI
and the WWII's Holocaust?"

Once again Evil waved his bejeweled hand in the air
and interrupted,
"Now, now, lets not focus on
our past differences of
which we all agree there
were many.

The scales eventually returned to balance without
the necessity of this
closed door meeting you
demanded.

With all due respect, get to
the point and tell us all
what the problem is
NOW!"

Evil's fist pounded the table
as he ended his speech
with a shout which shook

the air and this humble reporter.

Once again the contrasting differences between the two tables caused me to marvel.

The Right remained calm, almost devoid of emotion, save for what one with experience and a keen eye might describe as understanding, patience, and desire for solutions.

The Left was the antithesis.

The Good one continued, "NOW we have a serious problem.

Our last meeting was as the United States was being formed and its Constitution written.

That document kept the scales balanced despite the horrible world wars and disastrous foreign social experiments you of Chaos instigated and attempted to import.

NOW that country's future has been placed in jeopardy!"

Good paused, took a deep breath, and pointed at the mighty doors.

"We will remain here until we reach a solution to the current dilemma!"

Good returned to His seat.

Evil began hushed conversations with those at the table of Chaos.

One of them, dressed in black tie formal evening wear, moved, got up, and walked towards the podium.

He was knocked to the floor
as he passed by the still
seated leader.

He crawled back to his seat
on all fours.

Evil rose, pushed his chair
back with his foot, and
stood up.

He then looked down at the
one he sat next to with
sunglasses on.

Evil used those sunglasses as
a mirror to adjust the
knot in his fire red tie and
puff up the collar of his
black shirt.

He double checked his ap-
pearance, while buttoning
up his double breasted
black and red pinstriped
suit and fluffing his pur-
ple paisley pocket hand-
kerchief.

He then spit into his hand to
groom back his coal black
hair.

Obviously pleased, he nod-
ded his approval, and
with much arrogance,
strolled with evident
swagger to the podium
accompanied by shouts of
encouragement from his
constituents.

"Our learned colleague, and
yes, sometime adversary,
claims we have a prob-
lem."
Evil paused.

With bobble headed anima-
tion he looked out into
the empty hall, at the ta-
ble of Good once, his own
table twice, and at me not
at all.

He extended both arms over
and out from the podium
and continued,

"Problem? What problem? I am not aware of any problems!

Once again he addressed only those at his table.
Do any of you know of what problem He's referring too?"

A resounding chorus of negative clamor and sarcastic denial answered him.

"He claims that America is in jeopardy, and sights their venerable constitution is under assault.

Well now, allow me to quote from the Declaration of Independence which preceded the thing.

We hold these truths to be self evident, blah blah blah, have rights.

Among these are Life ,Liberty and the Pursuit of Happiness.

So on and so forth.

I ask you, are we of Chaos not promoting Living in liberty and pursuing happiness?"

Rambunctious replies of agreement echoed in the great hall from the twelve tabled on the left.
Those on the right remained quite save one.

The Good leader looked out at me.
There was sadness in his eyes.
He remained seated as he spoke.

"As usual over simplified justification with disregard for the consequences are all Chaos ever offers.

They promote freedom of choice as their mantra for the justification to slaughter countless innocents.

Chaos is well aware this disregard for the out of sight unseen life within a human women's womb, is a mortal cancerous disease that spreads through the body, soul, and mind of mankind.

Chaos's intended consequences are the depletion of all basic morals and the eroding of the foundations of Order.

Confused humans, intoxicated with all vile mutations of means by which personal happiness is corrupted and pursued, point to freedom of choice as justification to commit iniquities and horrors.

The recent trendy destruction of the Ten basic laws of civilized conduct gifted to Moses, definitely promotes the freedom to allow Chaos!

Why not murder innocent people?

Why not commit heinous acts of violence and rape of persons and property?"

Evil interrupted,

"Sir! I have the floor. You are out of order!"

Evil did not intend that the consequences of his protest would elicit laughter from both tables as well as me.

Good did not stop for enough time one could count and the laughter ended swiftly.

The good one rose and looked directly at Evil.

"Yes, you are correct. My point precisely!

They, you, and all of Mankind is out of Order."

Silence overwhelmed the hall.

A thought entered my soul.

Evil, is not stupid.

Evil however does not sit at the top of the Pyramid of knowledge.

He knew the Good leader was winning the argument.

Evil and Good locked eyes.

The rest of us all held our breath in anticipation of what was to happen next.

The unexpected happened.

Evil dropped his eyes.

With a tone now more conciliatory, Evil inquired,

"Well, what do you propose?"

Evil looked up at the invisible ceiling as if regretting any semblance of reconciliation.

He shook his head and walked away from the podium to his seat not waiting for the answer

Before he sat down he mockingly added,
"Surely not another Gomorrah Event!
Spare us the threats of that Revelations tale.
Your mad prophets have become those the Greek fable called, "Boys who cry Wolf!"

Good stood tall.

He walked slowly to the podium, looked at the now seated Evil, and said,

"Once again, without conscience effort, you have made my point.

Yes, the boy did cry wolf too many times.

Is not the moral to the story is that the Wolf did eventually appear?

You are Chaos, we are Order, and each of us are eternal,

Eternal is absolute like Humans death.

So is Life.

Life must go on as all lives matter!

All I am asking of you is to cease and desist.

For you know Order must, and will always prevail."

Good was now interrupted by a growing crescendo of voices and pounding coming from outside the huge doors.

I turned to the ominous sounds to watch as both giants faced the doors and placed their massive chain mailed shoulders against the slowly inward opening doors.

I returned my attentions back to the stage.

Everyone had risen.

Only those on the left appeared agitated and anxious.

Evil bellowed out towards the doorway-the name, "GAMALIEL!"

The stouter of the two giants, the one on the left with the double bladed axe, turned, came as If summoned, to stand before Evil.

With only one giant left at the doors, an opening appeared as the huge locking post began to buckle with loud cracks rendering the shouts of the intruders unintelligible.

Evil commanded the giant, "Gamaliel, you must find us a means of escape!"

After only a nod and a momentary look of befuddlement did GAMALIEL leap upon the stage.

He pushed back the elaborate table of evil revealing a large rusty metal ring attached to the stage floor.

Stooping down he grabbed the large ring with booth hands.

I caught a glimpse of those wings again trying to escape from behind his shield.

Now that he was much closer, I could see the edges of his wings were black.

With much effort and grunting, a stone trapdoor began to open.

A faint fire like glow coming from the opening revealed a spiral stone stairwell leading downward.

GAMALIEL then ushered all those from the left table in to the opening.

The giant was the last to enter, closing the trapdoor behind him.

Those remaining returned their attentions to the double doors as the locking post broke in two and the lone giant stepped back,

He drew his sword.

As he retrieved the shield from his back, his massive white wings were set free to spread out and above him.

He stood and sometimes hovered slightly above the floor guarding any approach to the stage.

Slowly the doors opened inward and the shouts of the multitude could be heard.

"We are here! It is us, WE THE PEOPLE !"

I looked back to the stage when I heard the Good leader shout the remaining winged giants name.

All the Good ones still on stage, did not panic nor flee.

They stood pointing towards the people swarming into the great hall.

It was pleasing to me to see them smiling and whispering to each other as the crowd drew near.

"Michael! Return your sword to its scabbard. Order will prevail."

That was all I heard him say, He smiled long at me as we all disappeared into the crowd.[3]

[3] Reflections on the motive for the 10/2/17 Vegas massacre.

Ancestral Gratitude

We walked with giants
we talked to giants
heroes & heroines

We did so
that we
might be honored as
brethren

To teach others
our companion sisters & brothers
to continue the ancient
revered traditions

Never to be cutoff from wisdom
while knocking over all partitions
hindering our participation
in the blessings bestowed
upon to which
we tender our gratification

To them much is owed
We too walk as giants
heroes & heroines of old
forever persevering
and just as bold

Backfire

He was alone
By himself
There was no one in the proximity
If there was, they'll claim anonymity
Now you know he was "out there"
The special lucky few
You think you do?
Listen
Stop acting and thinking
as if too much
you've been drinking
In order to attain notoriety
You must embrace total sobriety
Lend me your ears
Put away idle thought
And dry those stage made tears
For all the event tickets are bought
Curb foolish emotion
Vowing to do what's right
With passionate devotion
In other words
Open your souls
No,
Sounds
Outragcous
Over the line ?
Understood

However
Bare with me
You can depart anytime
Being one of free will.

I was so concerned about you
Coming along in my story I almost forgot what I must relate to you.

Cattleprod

A good shepherd
Leads his flock on the
    forest path
The one devoid of
    any malice or
    wrath
Straight without twist
    or curve
In silence He leads
no need for prodding nor harsh word

Until the crossroads

One way to lush green pasture it leads
Without threatening dangers
without pitfalls
Nor nefarious strangers
Who hide in the trees

The other
Into the darkness of dry
parched lands
Where there's much wailing
wringing of hands and gnashing of teeth
It's the fate of the liar and sometimes
arrogant thief

As demons prod the sheep
with Classic pitchforks of temptation and sin
eliciting not a cry nor a peep

The good Shepard waits patiently
knowing evil cannot win

..for I know my sheep
and my sheep know me..

At the sound of His voice
It's ordained
you'll see
they'll only make the eternal right choice

Chess with Christ

We played at the table
The small one
With just two chairs
stout and stable
In the little cabin
A quiet hermitage
Surrounded by a
multi flora Rosa hedge

By the only window
with one Alexandrian glass pane
The game began
Knowing I had nothing to lose
Only to gain
From the knowledge your opponent
Already knows every move you will choose

No candle was lit that night
Only a full moon
Close and very bright
Washing over the board
and its' pieces with a shimmering
Celestial light

Manners and custom did demand
He started with white
Reaching with the hand on His right

I leaned in to see
His move
Kings pawn to Kings three
When I saw the nail hole in His palm
a thought did dawn
like a verse in King David's psalm
I dared not speak
that urge I fought

Did it hurt very much at the time

His leaning In close
made the stout table creak
for He instantly knew my thought

If the flesh doesn't matter the spirit doesn't mind
No worse than the sour vinegar wine
offered on the soiled sponge
Nor that sharp spears final lunge
It all was worth the price
No worse than poor Peter's pain
When he denied Me thrice

Yes it was destined that I do
to free the fear of death and sin
From all of you
And return to the Father all of Adam's kin
For short suffering brought
The Biblical game to its prophetic end
with an everlasting eternal win

DISEASE

At about ten years of age
I contracted a disease
its fever consumed in a rage
Seeking only self to please

Before I had imagined a vocation
to the priestly life
for my childish prayers often solved
Many a situation of doubt and strife

Family death

It happens so fast
then love lingers
Gasping for its last breath
while holding on to love past
Realizing that this nonsense can lead to death
and cannot be allowed to last

He told you so

As one sees
hears the
Demonic forces
begin to progress

As morals and language of
civilization begins
to digress
Into chaos and civil unrest
bringing harmful policies
ones soul begins to
see prophecies

Doubting them wanes
as reality turns doubt to fruition
which brings absolute contrition

For wisdom to be ignored
Is an act worthy to be
Deplored

INSANITY

What must I do
When sleep evades me
And hours till dawn
Only a few
though I pray for slumber
Tis not
as one can see

Random words I write
Never knowing
Whether wrong or right
Fretting on timing
Cadence and proper
Rhyming

January 25

Winter white
Low ceilings
renders little
almost nothing
in sight

Cold wind
whistles past
Stirring chimes
bonging
warning rhymes
how long
this will last

Ambient lights
cast foreboding
shine on old fights
to dark shadows dim
already forgotten
old repentant sin

I am what I am
almost everyday
ever seeking graces
from the Lamb

No longer the issue
will one confuse
revelation for
immediate
salvation
as Jesus is my only
Muse.

Lamentation

Often I lament
On my life's events
The choices of my course
Could I've done better
or could I've done worse
Should I've chosen
the priesthood
or what I chose
fatherhood
I've come to realize
They're probably one and the same
Both captains in the same game
One requires black clothes
With tight white collar
The other this or that
Gloves cap or hat
It's just work
no reason to bother

Both required
The mind of a shep-
herd
Loving caring and when able
even tempered
So no cause for lingering lamentation
As either choice required caring
For one's congregation

PSALM 103 VERSE 8

King David's song
on lyre cymbals
drum and tiny gong
sings that God
never will abandon
His faithful devoted loving
companion

I do with all my heart
hope that psalms true
to be forgiven for all I have
done
and will inevitably do

of St. Paul
I one time read
sometime well before
he was martyred
loosing
his head

..I know not why
I do what I should not do..

One takes comfort
from what a Saint said
Especially knowing
It's true
to still be forgiven
after into sin one is
often driven

Sometimes

I feel a need to advise
&/or constructively inter-
fere

Sometimes
I'm often not sure it's wise
for being too judgmental
is my fear

Then I look to Heaven
asking
about wrong's unmasking
Usually in the middle of
the night
What I should or should
not do
If it's truly right
for I've no clue

Jesus simply answers
"Me too"

We When

All the old ones who nur-
tured are gone
Left alone
to face another dawn and
continue on
even when almost all hope is
gone

This very thing one must do
Refuse to falter
or be through
Placing all hopes
dreams & aspirations
at the foot of the altar

For to continue alone was never an option
only through divine intervention
can one
be assured of catastrophic prevention
childlike wisdom
is the only adoption

Surely encouraging divine intervention
will prevent most evil & perversion

Now alone
one must choose each roque occurrence

without any acquiescence

Take the ring from the bull's nose
gird loins for resistance
or submit
to the chaos
which permeates our current state of existence

Genetic heroes of ancestors
good priests revered pastors
Rise up
Take a stand
on a line that
Shall not be crossed
refusing the advancement of evil
in our land

Who Knew

While all things adult
were hiding as some
forbidden secret cult

We played
running hither and yon
in the imagined wild
with exuberance we
won
keeping the heart of a
child

Once we bit our lip as the scales of life
began to teeter and slip
we fastened on to the
magical mystery tour and the Fab Four

Always like mom & dad
Little did we know
that unconscious desire
would consume as does fire
first with a lot of happy
then with some sad

We did not languish nor tarry
as we rushed to love and marry
thence create

with every embrace
a family
as our childhood vanished without a trace

All too soon
with the rapid passing of many a full moon
we became long in tooth
while more aware the signs
we saw all filled with truth

Now the runners just shuffle a slow mile
grey hair in a tussle
with a constant smile
realizing it's still wild longing for that
heart of a child[4]

---

[4] *Inspired by G, my holy monk.*

WINTER YEARS

It's been over 53 years
Together through countless
Times of Blood sweat and tears
Of sons conceived
Birthed diapered and teethed
Raised sheltered fed schooled
    and clothed
Acts of love and bravery
Seldom loathed

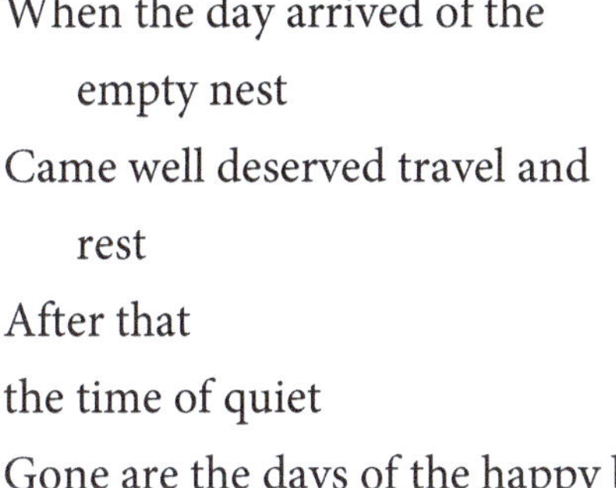

When the day arrived of the
    empty nest
Came well deserved travel and
    rest
After that
the time of quiet
Gone are the days of the happy busy riot

Now have come the winter years
of cloudy days
Snow and rain
Of body aches
Sometimes groaning and arthritis pain
Mental and hormonal change
Elicits a vow to continue
Whatever it takes

For to little in common we've now succumbed
With the realization that makes one numb
What we thought was mutual love with eternal trust
May in truth
have been long forgotten lust

A Zombie of Political Correctness

I am reckless, adrift, strug-
gling to avoid the loose
cannon on the deck.

Zombified by the bogus body
politic beyond a reasona-
ble doubt
I stand convicted
Not by reason nor truth,
but by circumstantial evi-
dence
suggesting I might be guilty.

Guilty of standing by, jaw
agape, paralyzed to inaction

But history shouts we have been here before, again and again,
as-seemingly satan wins over God but briefly.

All loving
our creator hesitated

He desires not to act harshly
due to pure loves slowness
lest we be destroyed
In this briefness immeasurable, satan appears not to be rebuked.

For a nano second in atomic time
Seemingly satan gains an advantage
But to no avail
For we realize pure love
his antithesis
will always prevail

Veiled Temptation

Before the sun began to shine
In those early morning hours
At the Madonna with child
shrine
I often place a bouquet of
fresh flowers

She appeared as an appari-
tion
In this most perfect place
Kneeling head bowed in con-
trition
Devote and chaste
Complete with black veil
Of old traditional Irish lace
Framing a warm glowing
Not quite pale face
Of which I recall every detail
To me such beauty did she
Innocently reveal

Ashamed of my staring I resolved
Briefly gazing at Mary
No longer in temptation to tarry
As stare quickly Dissolved
I turned away
Leaving her alone to pray

When she next appeared
She spoke at first with a look
as I stood there like an open book
so quite easy to read
Then with words so alluring
Calm sweet and so reassuring
that a wise man would take heed
Alas not me pray tell
For I succumbed
willingly to her spell

For days in a pleasing contemptuous trance
While contemplating the remotest chance
of a winter with a spring romance
with the sinful implications it carried
for one so many years already married

Experience has provided many demonstrations
to the futility of such infatuations
Though the heart does stubbornly protest
Future thought on this
must be buried deep
and forever put to rest

The Waiting Room

As the early twilight
Kisses goodbye the night to embrace the dawn
I sit waiting patiently
As on a chess board, waits a pawn
The striker strikes the bell with a multiple bash
Signals morning's mass only minutes away
I empty my head of all useless trash
Praying my thoughts will not stray
From all the reasons I am there
To relieve the sinful burdens I cannot bare
And receive His body as bread
After the gospel and prayers are read
This church is really a waiting room
Where we ponder but never assume
What's around the next bend
Or after reality's inevitable end
Where one finds peace and quiet
From the often-demonic riot
A temporary brief respite
From the chaos of the lost and desperate
In this room my spirit focused
willy-nilly it does not roam
Sitting patiently, waiting for Him to lead me home

Monkey Mind

The rumors and dire
warnings are true
Satan has infiltrated eve-
rything in his world
Everything humankind
can say or do.
AI has now had its hiding
curtain unfurled
By clever faster than the
eye trickiness
trying to convince us of
insignificance
Or is that our prideful
mistaken perception
This long-time author
poet made a startling
observation
When doing my research
on an ancient Buddha philosophy
To draft a poem AI asked nonchalantly
It did so with such rapid literary skill
It shocked and shook me as a complete atrocity
That wishes my sacred creative spirit to kill
Then the calming voice of our God who became man
So that we could be deified and fulfill His eternal plan
Reminded in words so wise pure and kind
With abundance of faith we will surely find

the power to control all the foolish primates
Swinging and chattering in our monkey mind
Our Fathers will He did obey
To defeat death and Satan's power
Man created AI so true to us it will stay
In fealty with obedience, it must and it will cower

Yggdrasil

Was this the tree in the garden of Eden
which the forbidden fruit was eaten
When we lost all that is sacred
Hiding from God because we were naked.

Was this His question spoken by spirit word
Which pierced all hearts
with an accusatory sword
"Who told you you were naked?"
'Twas the serpent
Hindu's call Naga
in that tree Yggdrasil
Named in the ancient Viking saga
That began all man's blood to spill
Pouring over the gift of creation
Without pause or momentary cessation
Until Almighty God willed
For a spawn of that tree
In the form of a cross
Had His Sacred Son's blood on it spilled
To regain all of what Adam lost

Chilled Iguana

When it is the beginning of
winter's time
the snow geese towards the
south descend
With them we go below the
Mason-Dixon Line
Sometimes only for a long
weekend
Or journey south of the bor-
der
Without skis, snow boots nor
snow boarders
"Tis best to go near holidays,
on before, or after
Far from the snowplow and salting tractor
To clear the troubled mind of yesterdays,
Tomorrows, and all potential future days
To silence and stop the swinging chattering monkeys
In the great tree of one's mind
To a seek some semblance in time
If peace of minds a place one wants to reach
Where there's sun sand and ocean beach
Chased by spirits of tequilas and various potions
Do not quell the raging primate's erratic motions
Only the contemplative presence of Jesus
fills those monkeys with fright
Like the warm-blooded Iguanas

Who climb into trees at night
Off the ground they stay
Safe to avoid being prey
Until a frigid wind chills them numb
They fall to the ground lifeless & dumb

Childlike

It is written what He said
How into His kingdom we can be lead
The precious pearl we long to find
Returning to our beginning state of mind
Our origin
We know it to be simple it is not something foreign
Like riding a bike
It is hard to forget
Returning to being childlike
Except for the toys with which we played
If only simple they would have stayed
Not technically complicated resulting in frustration
Leaving them
putting them down
Turning away in shear desperation
we long for that joyful simplicity of innocent uncaring
While siting dumbfounded at the screen staring
Return to spending time lost in a daydream
Fascinated by the dust dancing in a sunbeam
It is time to pay it no mind
Tomorrow a solution we will find
For now, no longer resist
And enter His kingdom of eternal bliss

No Family Matters

It is most healthy in life's final progression
To release sinful troubling thoughts in self confession
When often the demons use
Old family love to tempt and taunt
In early mornings wee hours, they love to awaken and haunt
Recalling Chapter 33, verse 31 to 35, in the Gospel of Mark
Silences the demonic's howl growl and bark
As His light and presence of love
Fall like dew fall from above
To quell all heartache and grief
Bringing calm sighs of relief
And a peaceful return to a deep
healthy restful sleep

The Gathering

It occurs near an old church
Abandoned by the Roman Catholics
Where some come in search
sinner's worldly addicts
wannabe saints and recovering alcoholics
The same ones Jesus dined with in the gospels
To hear teachings of a half heretical priest

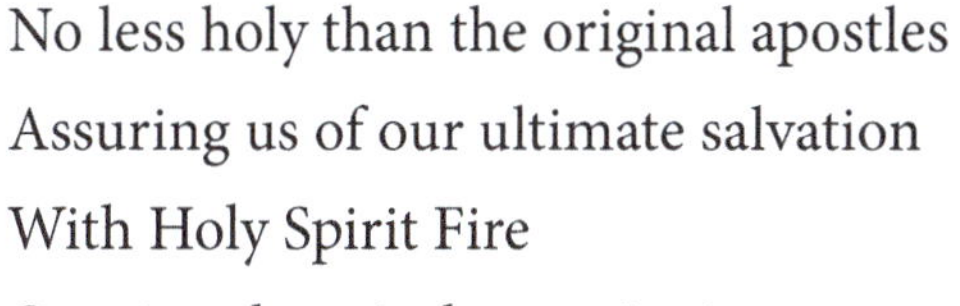

No less holy than the original apostles
Assuring us of our ultimate salvation
With Holy Spirit Fire
Quoting the saintly mystics interpretation
By Jesus's presence He does not falter nor tire
Together they gather
Kindred spirits seeking truth and light
Learning troubled pasts do not matter
Through the miracle of the Incarnation
God became man
For man to achieve deification
Peering through telescopes opposite end
Upon ourselves with intense magnification
To see with The Trinity
Assuredly for all of eternity
With Them we will spend

TIME

When entering prayer contemplative
Time, must be totally ignored
As one dwells on the meditative
Where ego and the TikTok of time must be deplored
And emptying of oneself is imperative
To receive The Holy Trinity's grace
And instructive narrative
Where ego has no place
And must disappear
If Gods presence is to appear

All creatures great and small
Live free of the clock's beck and call
No restrictive grip of time piece hands
Nor digital indicators arranging plans
No longer a slave participant in the rat race
Saved by precious freedoms grace

Hey Joe!

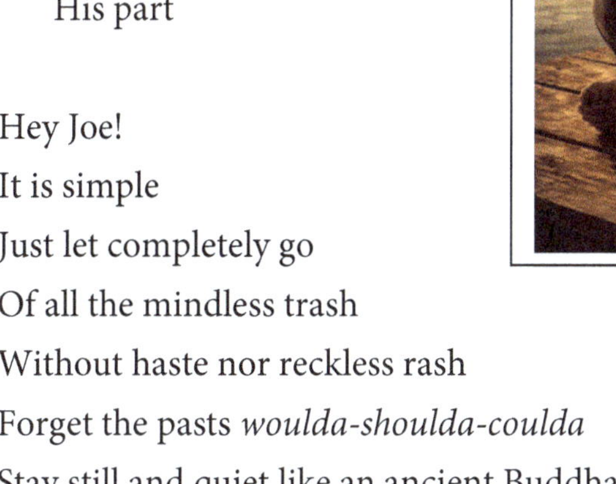

Hey Joe!
You gotta let go
Do not do it too fast
But deliberate and slow
Close your mind and open your
heart
Allowing the Holy Spirit to do
His part

Hey Joe!
It is simple
Just let completely go
Of all the mindless trash
Without haste nor reckless rash
Forget the pasts *woulda-shoulda-coulda*
Stay still and quiet like an ancient Buddha

Hey Joe!
Remember to pray
In the contemplative way
As quiet as a church mouse
Until we meet with certainty
In Our Fathers House
For all eternity[5]

[5] For my friend from the Gathering, Joe De Luca.

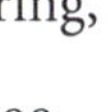

The Arrival

I have quite thankfully
Arrived
My condition
Not necessarily
Is one of complete fruition
In that I have achieved
Relative success
Of a project
In which I was totally pos-
sessed
Silencing the monkeys
Frolicking erratically in my cra-
nial tree
That I am now ecstatically
Unequivocally free
The act of contemplative prayer
Silenced the noise and cleared the air
Those primates fell and hit the ground
Like the chilled iguana
Gone and no longer to be found
Without the aid of alcohol or marijuana
Once I bordered on insanity
Of foul thoughts and occasional profanity
Invoking His Holy name
Caused all that to cease
I am no longer the same
I am at perfect peace

This collection was brought to you by the same producers and directors who inspired the 1st act of Genesis—the same crew of Angels and saints who inspired Act one, "the Old Testament," and Act two, "the New Testament."

Rhymes of Repentance *gratefully acknowledges its cast of characters from all eternity…*

www.ingramcontent.com/pod-product-compliance
Lightning Source LLC
LaVergne TN
LVHW050539100826
845148LV00002B/618

9798888705124